COUNTDOWN TO SPACE

JOHN GLENN RETURNS TO ORBIT
Life on the Space Shuttle

Carmen Bredeson

Series Advisor:
John E. McLeaish
Chief, Public Information Office, retired,
NASA Johnson Space Center

Enslow Publishers, Inc.

40 Industrial Road   PO Box 38
Box 398   Aldershot
Berkeley Heights, NJ 07922   Hants GU12 6BP
USA   UK

http://www.enslow.com

Copyright © 2000 by Carmen Bredeson

Library of Congress Cataloging-in-Publication Data

Bredeson, Carmen.
    John Glenn returns to orbit: life on the space shuttle / Carmen Bredeson.
        p. cm. — (Countdown to space)
    Includes bibliographical references and index.
    Summary: Describes the activities aboard the space shuttle Discovery during
its historic flight in 1998 when John Glenn, at age seventy-seven, returned to
space.
    ISBN 0-7660-1304-9
    1. Life support systems (Space environment)—Juvenile literature. 2. Space
flights—Juvenile literature. 3. Space shuttles—Juvenile literature. 4. Glenn, John,
1921—Juvenile literature. 5. Astronauts—United States—Juvenile literature.
[1. Space flights. 2. Space shuttles. 3. Glenn, John, 1921– 4. Astronauts.]
I. Title. II. Series.
TL1500.B75   2000
629.47'7—dc21
                                                                99-012490

Printed in the United States of America

10 9 8 7 6 5 4 3 2 1

To Our Readers: All Internet addresses in this book were active and appropriate
when we went to press. Any comments or suggestions can be sent by e-mail to
Comments@enslow.com or to the address on the back cover.

Photo Credits: National Aeronautics and Space Administration

Cover Illustration: NASA (foreground); Raghvendra Sahai and John
Trauger (JPL), the WFPC2 science team, NASA, and AURA/STScI
(background).

Cover photo: The crew of STS-95: (seated from left) Steven W. Lindsey
and Curtis L. Brown, Jr.; (standing from left) Scott F. Parazynski, Stephen
K. Robinson, Chiaki Mukai, Pedro Duque, and John H. Glenn, Jr.

CONTENTS

A fiery show of power lifts the Discovery shuttle off the launchpad, with "a crew of six astronaut heroes and one American legend."

1

Liftoff

At main-engines ignition, the space shuttle *Discovery* rumbled to life like a giant beast. As power built, eight bolts held the shuttle to the launch tower. Bursts of flame blasted into the solid rocket boosters, and more than one million pounds of solid fuel erupted into a blazing inferno. The explosive bolts were fired, and the shuttle was on its way! "Liftoff of *Discovery* with a crew of six astronaut heroes and one American legend," announced NASA commentator Lisa Malone.[1]

Thousands of eyes watched as the space shuttle *Discovery* roared into the blue sky over Florida. The roads and beaches around Kennedy Space Center were full of spectators who had come to see the October 29, 1998, launch. Millions more followed the liftoff on their television sets and radios. As *Discovery* rose into the sky, NBC's Tom Brokaw said on the air, "I don't know what your grandfather is doing today, but John Glenn is on his way to space."[2]

Thirty-six years earlier, John Glenn became the first American to orbit Earth on February 20, 1962, aboard *Friendship 7*. Now, at age seventy-seven, Glenn was part of the *Discovery* crew, and the world's oldest astronaut. When Glenn was asked whether he was more nervous before his flight in 1962 or before this one in 1998, he replied, "I think I was probably more nervous back in those days because we did not know much about

In a Mercury spacesuit, John Glenn first traveled into space in 1962 (left). He returned to orbit thirty-six years later as a payload specialist aboard the space shuttle Discovery.

spaceflight . . . we were sort of feeling our way and finding out what would happen to the human body in space. . . ."[3] "Doctors even thought that the human eyeball would change shape in weightlessness and we wouldn't see clearly," added Glenn.[4]

Two and a half minutes after launch, the solid rocket boosters had burned up their fuel and were jettisoned from *Discovery*. For the next six minutes, the shuttle continued to climb and increase its speed. Shuttle commander Curt Brown described what a shuttle liftoff feels like.

> We jump off the launchpad and accelerate right up to 2-1/2 Gs which means you would weigh 2-1/2 times what you weigh here on Earth. By the time we get up to orbital speed, we're up to around 3 Gs which means if you weighed 100 pounds on the ground, you would weigh 300 pounds during that ascent, so we do feel the Gs at acceleration.[5]

Astronaut Roberta Bondar described it another way. "Imagine lying on your back with a full-grown gorilla sitting on your chest."[6]

Eight and a half minutes into the flight, the main engines cut off and the astronauts were thrown forward in their seats. The empty liquid fuel tank dropped away, and the shuttle entered orbit around Earth, going 17,500 miles per hour. Suddenly all the pressures of acceleration were gone, and everything aboard the shuttle that was not tied down began to float. John Glenn and his crewmates were still strapped in their seats, not able to float just yet.

On his second trip into space aboard *Discovery*, John Glenn was not in command of the ship. He explained, "I'm a payload specialist. There are seven of us flying, and my name is not at the top."[7] Payload specialists are not career astronauts. Instead, they are people who have special skills for conducting research aboard the space shuttle. Mission specialists are NASA astronauts who keep the shuttle operating systems running smoothly. Included in this group are the mission commander and pilot.

The Discovery *crew boards the van that will take them to the launchpad.*

An artist's cutaway view of the space shuttle shows the cockpit above the mid-deck crew cabin. Spacehab is in the payload bay.

The *Discovery* mission was also known as STS-95, which stands for Space Transportation System and the number assigned to the flight. The entire *Discovery* crew included commander Curt Brown, who was five years old when John Glenn first orbited Earth in 1962; pilot Steve Lindsey; mission specialists Scott Parazynski, Pedro Duque, and Stephen Robinson; and payload specialists Chiaki Mukai and John Glenn.

2

In Orbit

Once *Discovery* reached orbit, pilot Steve Lindsey turned the shuttle over and pointed its nose toward Earth. In this position the crew was able to see Earth from the cockpit windows. The astronauts unhooked their harnesses and floated gently out of their seats. During their orbit of Earth, astronauts are essentially free-falling all the time. The astronauts feel weightless and float in the shuttle.

Shuttle commander Curt Brown was watching to see John Glenn's reaction to feeling weightless. He reported to Mission Control, "Let the record show John has a smile on his face, and it goes from one ear to the other one."[1] Glenn said to those on Earth, "Zero G, and I feel fine."[2] On Glenn's first mission in 1962, he was strapped into the seat of his tiny Mercury capsule and not able to really experience the feeling of weightlessness.

One of the first things shuttle astronauts like to do after reaching orbit is look out of the windows at Earth. John Glenn had a conversation with Mission Control about what he saw from *Discovery*.

Glenn: "We are just going by Hawaii, and that is absolutely gorgeous."

Mission Control: "Roger that, glad you are enjoying the show."

Glenn: "Boy, enjoying the show is right. This is beautiful."[3]

After getting a quick look at Earth, the astronauts had to go to work. First they folded up the two extra seats in the shuttle cockpit and three seats in the mid-deck crew cabin and stored them out of the way. There was now room to change out of their launch/entry suits and into the clothes they would wear during the mission.

Each crew member had on board enough pants, shirts, underwear, and sleep shorts to last for the length of the mission. The astronauts' work clothes are much like the ones we wear on Earth, except they are fire retardant and have pockets everywhere. Since things float away in Earth orbit, the astronauts need lots of pockets to hold their tools, pens, glasses, and snacks.

Shoes are not needed on board the shuttle because nobody needs to walk. Instead, the astronauts wear socks, soft slippers, or just go barefoot. The astronaut

Astronauts Scott Parazynski and Stephen Robinson check the house-keeping system inside the shuttle. The astronauts do not need shoes on the shuttle, and they place their feet in foot restraints to stay in one place.

crew quarters are pressurized and have a supply of oxygen, much like the cabin of an airplane, so face masks and pressure suits are not needed while astronauts are working inside.

In order to move around in the shuttle, astronauts must push off gently from the walls. Too hard a push sends them crashing into the opposite wall. Astronaut Robert Crippen, who flew on the first shuttle mission in 1981, said, "At first I did things that surprised me, like shoving off from one side of the mid-deck a bit too hard and finding myself sprawled on the opposite wall."[4]

The astronauts' posture is affected by weightlessness, too. Arms float out in front of the body, and all of the joints bend slightly. The spine stretches out, too, and most astronauts are about an inch taller while in orbit. John Glenn explained that floating around was a new experience for him. "I didn't do that before because in Project Mercury, the spacecraft there was just big enough that you were strapped into it, and all you could do was loosen the straps a little bit and there was no place to float to."[5]

Being in space actually weakens the bones and muscles because they do not have to work as hard as they did on Earth. Exercising on a treadmill or using a rowing machine helps the astronauts keep their bodies strong. They cannot use the exercise equipment exactly the same way as they did on Earth, though. They must

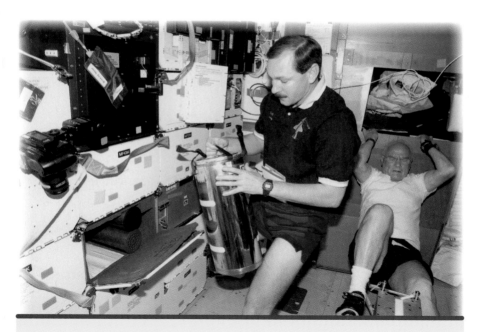

Commander Curt Brown takes an experiment out of a locker while John Glenn exercises during the shuttle flight.

attach belts and straps to their bodies to keep from floating off the machines.

There are also changes in the astronauts' appearance in space. On Earth, gravity pulls blood and fluids down into the legs. The legs work hard to keep fluid moving from the lower body to the upper body and brain. This process continues in space. But without the effects of gravity to balance the fluid, more of the fluid stays in the upper body in space. The astronauts' faces get puffy-looking. John Glenn said, "Everyone has a fluid shift up here, me included. The fluid shift comes up to your head and makes your face look a little more round."[6] Shifting body fluids make some astronauts sick for a couple of days. Usually, by the third day in space, the nausea goes away.

When John Glenn was asked if he had suffered any nausea, he replied, "Well, I guess I came up expecting to be a little bit nauseous. I think there's something like 65 or 70 percent of the people that come up have some sort of problems with stomach awareness, if we want to call it that or worse, and I haven't had any of that so far."[7]

In spite of some bouts of space sickness, there is no time to waste on a shuttle mission. The *Discovery* crew had a schedule packed full of experiments, housekeeping chores, maintenance, and food preparation. There were even a few hours thrown in for relaxation and sleep.

With the extra seats and suits stowed, there was room to move around in the crew cabin. The cabin is thirteen feet by fifteen feet. Astronaut Sally Ride, the first American woman to fly in space, said,

> The two rooms inside the shuttle seem much larger than they do on Earth, because we are not held down to the floor. We can use every corner of the room, including the ceiling. While one of us works strapped to a wall, another sits on the ceiling eating peanuts, and a third runs on a treadmill anchored to the floor.[8]

In the limited space of the crew cabin, there is a small bathroom that contains the shuttle's only toilet. Located behind a curtain, the toilet does not flush with water like the ones we use on Earth. Astronaut Mike Mullane explained, "Water won't flow in weightlessness, so it

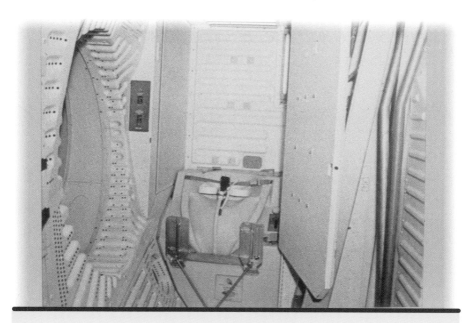

The toilet on the space shuttle uses air instead of water to remove waste.

can't be used in the space toilet. Instead, our space toilet uses air. Basically, astronauts go to the bathroom in a vacuum cleaner."[9]

In order to urinate, the astronaut attaches a personal funnel to a flexible hose, turns on the vacuum, and urinates into the funnel. To defecate, the astronaut sits on the toilet seat, attaches a seat belt and foot restraints to keep from floating away, and turns on the vacuum. Air suction pulls liquid and solid matter down into storage containers. After using the bathroom, each astronaut cleans up the area for the next person. Also located in the bathroom are lockers holding cloth towels and washcloths, paper towels, rubber gloves, disinfectant, and wet wipes.

The wall opposite the bathroom in the crew quarters is covered from top to bottom with large storage drawers. Clothing, food, tools, equipment, and science experiments are carried in these drawers. *Discovery* had eighty-three payloads, or experiments, on board, weighing a total of twenty-two thousand pounds. Many of the payloads were carried in a Spacehab module, a ten-foot-by-thirteen-foot portable laboratory located in the shuttle's payload bay. The payload bay is about the size of one and a half school buses.

Spacehab takes up about a quarter of the space in the sixty-foot-long payload bay. Spacehab is not included on all missions, but can be added if there is room available. It provides extra working space for two astronauts and

Payload specialist Chiaki Mukai works with a plant sprout experiment onboard Discovery.

carries racks of experiments and storage lockers. The Spacehab module is pressurized, so the astronauts can wear ordinary clothing when working there. It also has an air supply, lights, and power and is attached to the crew cabin by an airlock and short tunnel. When working outside of Spacehab in the payload bay, astronauts must wear spacesuits since the area is exposed to outer space.

The *Discovery* crew had a full schedule of work to do during their nine-day mission. After setting up Spacehab and starting some of the experiments, the astronauts were ready to have their first shuttle meal.

3

Eating, Cleaning, and Sleeping

Months before liftoff, the *Discovery* astronauts tasted samples of more than one hundred foods at NASA. Each crew member then selected a menu for every day during the mission. Different colored dots for each astronaut were placed on the food containers. John Glenn's food packages were marked with a purple dot, and Curt Brown's had a red dot. Shrimp cocktail was a favorite food for many of the astronauts. John Glenn said, "The shrimp cocktail they fix is very, very good. . . . Curt likes shrimp and I always tell him that when he's on the flight deck and I'm hungry, I'm going to go looking for a red dot."[1]

Tortillas are often used in place of bread on the shuttle because they do not crumble as easily as bread.

A Typical Day's Menu

Breakfast	Lunch	Dinner
Dried Pears Scrambled Eggs Breakfast Roll	Ham Cheese Spread Tortillas Fruit Cocktail	Teriyaki Chicken Macaroni & Cheese Green Beans Brownie

Shuttle crews also have many drinks to choose from, including apple and grape juice, tea, cocoa, and coffee. All of the drinks are packaged in powdered form and must have water added before they are sipped through a straw. Snack foods, such as granola bars, nuts, cookies, candy, and containers of pudding, are also available for the crew.

When it is mealtime aboard *Discovery*, crew members take turns getting the food ready. Prior to the flight, the liquid has been taken out of some of the meals to make them easier to store. Before the food is eaten, hot or cold water is injected back into the package through a needle. While some of the food is heated in a small oven, trays are attached to the wall with Velcro. Utensils are placed on magnetic strips on the trays to keep them from floating away. Astronauts eat with a fork, spoon, and knife just as we do, but they also need scissors to cut open their food packages.

Ketchup, mayonnaise, and mustard come in small foil

Stephen Robinson and Pedro Duque make a sandwich with a tortilla.

packages like the ones from fast-food restaurants. But the little packages of salt and pepper we use on Earth do not work in space. If sprinkled in space, salt or pepper would float and get into the astronauts' eyes and noses. Salt is dissolved in water, and pepper suspended in oil, and squirted onto the food from a squeeze bottle.

Once the food packages are ready, they are placed on small Velcro squares on the trays to keep them in place. Each food package has one or two Velcro dots on the outside so it can be attached to the tray. When the crew gathers for a meal, they do not sit at a table, but float around the cabin with their food trays attached to their legs or to a wall. According to Commander Brown, "One of the more fun times of the orbiter life is when we all get together on mid deck and put our food together and tell stories and enjoy ourselves during the evening meal."[2]

Chewing and swallowing work the same way in space as they do on Earth. Digestion can be a little tricky during the first few hours in space, though. According to Curt Brown,

> When you get up here in space and you go into the weightlessness environment, your body is not sure what really just happened to it. So your stomach, intestines, and that stuff kind of shuts down for a few hours to figure out what is going on, and during that time frame your body is not doing much with your food. After your body figures out that it can handle the new environment, everything cranks back up and your food, stomach, and intestines all start working like normal.[3]

Just getting the food onto a spoon or fork and into the mouth can sometimes be tricky. A sudden move can launch food into the air. John Glenn told about eating one of his first shuttle meals. "I had some oatmeal and raisins. One little speck wound up on my glasses. I guess with old folks you normally think it falls down on an old man's necktie, but this time it wound up on my glasses."[4]

When the meal is finished, the astronauts put their empty cartons and packages into a trash bag and clean the trays and utensils with wet wipes. There is not a sink on the shuttle because water and soap would just float away. Crumbs are gathered up with a small vacuum. All of the crew members help keep the shuttle clean. It is a very small space and can get messy and dirty very quickly. The dry trash is placed in bags and put into storage bins in the crew cabin. The wet trash is also put in bags, but it is stored in the shuttle's third deck, an area that contains wires, pipes, and equipment.

The astronauts also have a hard time keeping themselves clean because there is no shower aboard the shuttle. When astronaut Mike Mullane was asked what he missed most in space, he replied: "A shower! After a lifetime of taking a daily shower or bath, going a week or two without one feels disgusting."[5]

In order to wash in space, water is squirted onto a washcloth and spread on the skin. Water does not drip off of the skin in space, but spreads out or floats. Soap is then rubbed onto the wet skin and wiped off with a different wet washcloth.

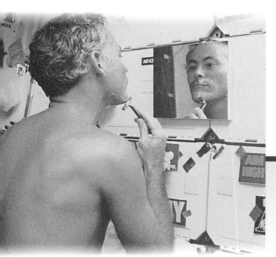

Shaving works just as well in space as on Earth. The sticky shaving cream traps whiskers so they don't float away. Then the shaving cream is wiped off with a wet washcloth.

Hair is washed using a shampoo that does not have to be rinsed. Since hair floats in space, it does not help much to comb it. Most female astronauts who have long hair keep it tied back and out of the way.

Brushing teeth is different in space because there is no sink in which to spit the toothpaste. Astronaut Dan Bursch said, "It may sound kind of gross, but some people actually swallow after they're through brushing their teeth, but most of the people end up just spitting it out into a towel or into a tissue and then we put that into a place we call the wet trash."[6]

When all of the chores and experiments are finished for the day, the *Discovery* astronauts have a little leisure time before bed. Some of the crew members write e-mail messages to their families at home; others read or listen to music on portable tape players. One of the favorite activities of orbiting astronauts is looking at Earth from the observation windows in the cockpit.

From the earliest days of space travel, astronauts have said that Earth is incredibly beautiful from space. With the shuttle traveling around Earth at five miles a second, the view is constantly changing. The shuttle does not orbit high enough to see the entire Earth at one time. Instead, the astronauts see only portions of the planet as it passes below them.

As John Glenn was looking out of the window while the shuttle passed over South Africa, a storm raged 345 miles below. Glenn said they saw "literally hundreds and hundreds of lightning flashes from many thunderstorms in different areas. I would say that all of them together, we probably saw six or seven hundred flashes."[7] Commander Brown said one of his biggest problems aboard the shuttle is ". . . getting everyone else to bed because you know if they go just a few feet and look out the window, they can see the beautiful Earth down below."[8]

Going to bed in space is very different from sleeping at home. For one thing, night does not last long in space. The shuttle orbits Earth once every ninety minutes. During one orbit, there are forty-five minutes of light

During their free time, astronauts enjoy watching the Earth from space. Here, a cyclone can be seen.

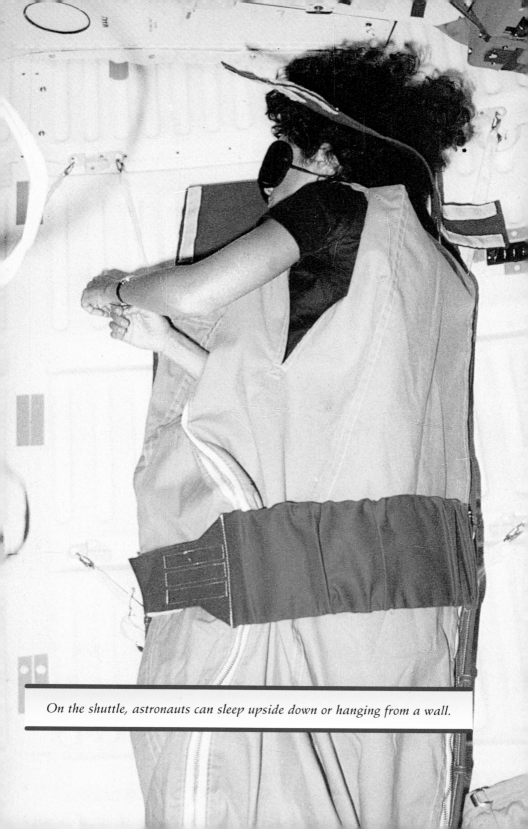

On the shuttle, astronauts can sleep upside down or hanging from a wall.

and forty-five minutes of darkness. In order to keep the light from shining in their eyes, many astronauts wear a black sleep mask. Some also wear earplugs to block out the noise around them.

Since there is no up or down in space, astronauts may sleep upside down or hanging from a wall. Their sleeping bags can be attached to any surface in the shuttle. While the astronauts are allotted eight hours for sleep each day, few manage to stay asleep that long. John Glenn said, "I don't know that you need quite the same amount of sleep up here. You are floating around and you aren't quite as tired."[9]

Excitement about being in space and the long list of tasks that have to be done may keep some astronauts from sleeping soundly, also. Commander Brown said that John Glenn "was happy to come fly with us, obviously. But he may not be happy after a few days in orbit. We plan to work him to the bone."[10] The work schedule for the *Discovery* crew was packed with enough to keep all seven crew members very busy.

4

Working and Relaxing

There are many experiments that can be performed in the weightlessness of space that cannot be done on Earth. Near-perfect crystals can be grown aboard the orbiting shuttle. Scientists and drug companies use the crystals to develop better medicine and treatments for disease. On STS-95, crystals of human insulin were grown and studied. After more research on Earth, scientists hope that the crystals can be used to make time-release insulin, which will help diabetics better control their blood sugar.

Some of the STS-95 experiments dealt with the way people age. By studying the way weightlessness affected John Glenn, scientists hoped to learn more about what happens to people as they get older. Glenn said, "We have some 34 million Americans that are over sixty-five right now and that figure . . . is going to be about 100 million by the year 2050."[1]

Elderly people on Earth suffer from a variety of problems that also affect astronauts in space, such as dizziness, sleep problems, muscle withering, bone loss, and immune system slowdown. Commander Brown explained, "Your immune system that keeps you healthy and fights off all the diseases that try to attack you—up in space that changes. Actually, it gets a little weaker. We are not sure why, but we are actually studying that here."[2]

In order to keep track of Glenn's physical condition, Scott Parazynski drew blood from the seventy-seven-year-old astronaut ten times during the mission. Glenn said, "Scott's taken my blood so many times that when I see him I say, 'Here comes Dracula.'"[3] Glenn added, "One disadvantage of the space shuttle is you can float, but you can't hide."[4]

Another test involving Glenn required him to swallow a large pill that contained a temperature sensor and a transmitter. The pill measured his internal temperature while he was working and sleeping. His sleep patterns were further monitored by twenty-one sensors that were attached to his head and body before bed. When Glenn was asked if the sensors bothered him, he replied, "It's really not that uncomfortable. You're weightless, so your head doesn't press down on the sensors."[5] Chiaki Mukai also wore sleep monitors so her

John Glenn gave blood samples ten times during the mission. The samples helped scientists track his physical condition during the trip.

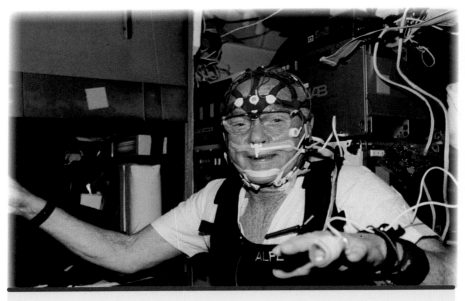

During a sleep study, sensors monitored John Glenn's sleep patterns.

responses could be compared with Glenn's. The sleep data was recorded on one of twenty laptop computers aboard *Discovery*. It took that many computers to keep track of all the experiments.

In addition to the laboratory experiments on board *Discovery*, the crew also had to deploy a Spartan satellite and retrieve it two days later. The Spartan was carried in the shuttle's payload bay. It was equipped with a pair of telescopes to study the Sun's corona and solar winds. The corona, or outer atmosphere of the Sun, reaches a temperature of 2 million degrees. Scientists hope that information gathered during STS-95 will help them better understand the Sun and its effect on Earth's climate.

All of the work with Spartan was done by remote control from within the shuttle, so the astronauts did not have to put on spacesuits for a spacewalk. Along the back wall of the cockpit there are instruments that are used to control the movements of the shuttle's fifty-foot-long robotic arm. Cameras located in the payload bay and on the robotic arm send pictures to two video monitors next to the instruments. There are also windows in the cockpit overlooking the payload bay. While watching the monitors, Steve Robinson used the computers and a joystick to pick up Spartan with the robotic arm and lift it into space.

After the successful launch of Spartan, Curt Brown reported, "This morning we had the opportunity to deploy the Spartan spacecraft. That went very, very well and it's now on its own, collecting science for the next two days."[6] John Glenn added, "It was a beautiful sight this morning to see that Spartan go out there. It was just, just beautiful. . . . I hope we bring back some good pictures."[7]

By day five of the STS-95 mission, the seven astronauts aboard *Discovery* were beginning to get a little tired. They were given a half day off to relax and enjoy being in space. Some took trips to the windows to look at Earth and outer space. The Moon, planets, and stars all appear to be the same size from the shuttle as they do from Earth. That is because the shuttle is not that much closer to them than we are on Earth. There are more stars visible from the shuttle, though. On Earth, air pollution and the atmosphere block the light of many stars from ever reaching our eyes.

When not looking out of the windows during leisure time, some astronauts entertain themselves by playing with food. One of their favorite games is batting M&Ms around and catching them in their mouths. Another fun game is slurping up blobs of water or juice that have been set loose to float around. Also, half-peeled bananas are sometimes sent spinning across the crew cabin with

Mission specialist Pedro Duque and pilot Steven Lindsey take a break from their busy schedule.

their peels sticking out like propeller blades. Some mission commanders ban bananas on the shuttle, though, because they smell so strong as they ripen.

John Glenn joined in the fun during free time. In addition to doing some somersaults he said, "We did some things like make balls of water that float out in front that you can inject with air bubbles."[8] The *Discovery* crew also got to visit with their families back on Earth by taking turns using a laptop computer that transmitted pictures and sound. Once the fun and games were over, the astronauts had to get back to work.

One of the items on the agenda was retrieval of the Spartan satellite. Curt Brown and Steve Lindsey maneuvered *Discovery* under and behind the three-thousand-pound satellite. While watching the monitors from inside the cockpit, Stephen Robinson carefully reached out with the robotic arm. He edged closer and closer to the satellite and then reported to Mission Control, "Houston, we've got a good grapple of Spartan."[9] He eased the 9-million-dollar satellite into the payload bay and locked it into place. During its two-day orbit, Spartan had taken twelve hundred images of the Sun for scientists on Earth to study.

When astronauts actually work out in the open payload bay or in space, they have to wear special space suits called extravehicular mobility units, or EMUs. The suits protect the astronauts from extreme temperatures, radiation, and the vacuum of space. Although there was

Stephen Robinson used the robotic arm (right) to retrieve the Spartan satellite from space. Spartan took over one thousand images of the Sun.

no spacewalk scheduled for the STS-95 mission, there were two crew members who were trained to do an extravehicular activity (EVA) in case an emergency arose.

Many shuttle missions have included EVAs. In 1993, astronauts successfully repaired the Hubble Space Telescope. During a week of spacewalks, the crew of *Endeavour* corrected Hubble's optical problems. Since that time, the telescope has sent amazing pictures back to Earth.

As the STS-95 crew worked day after day, the clock was slowly winding down on their mission. All too soon, it was time to stow the gear, put the orbiter in order, and head for home.

5

Return to Earth

During the STS-95 mission, the astronauts lost about 20 percent of their blood plasma volume, because the body does not need as much fluid in space. In order to build up their blood volume in preparation for their return, or entry, the astronauts drank as much liquid as they could. They also took salt tablets to help their bodies retain the fluid. While they were forcing water down, the crew members got into their launch/entry suits and strapped themselves into their seats.

Pilot Steve Lindsey turned *Discovery* around and pointed its tail in the direction it was moving. He then fired the engines to slow the shuttle, and gravity started to pull it out of orbit. Onboard computers directed all of the movements so that they were precise. The shuttle must begin its return to Earth at exactly the right moment in order to reenter and land successfully. As the shuttle began to enter Earth's atmosphere, it was turned around again, this time with the nose pointed forward.

Inside the shuttle, the first signs of gravity appeared when debris started drifting down on the astronauts. M&Ms, bits of food, and lost tools gently rained down from where they had been hiding in the nooks and crannies of *Discovery*. As the shuttle got closer and closer to Earth, the astronauts started feeling heavy. It was hard for them to even lift their arms since they were used to being weightless. Outside the cockpit windows, an

At the end of a successful nine-day mission, the crew of STS-95 got ready to head home.

orange glow filled the sky from the red-hot tiles on the shuttle exterior. Friction from Earth's atmosphere heated up the tiles and caused the shuttle to vibrate slightly.

When *Discovery* was about ten miles above Earth, commander Curt Brown and pilot Steve Lindsey took control of the shuttle from the computers. At this point, *Discovery* had no power of its own and was falling like a big glider. The shuttle falls at an angle six times greater than an airliner does during landing. There is no way to correct its course once the descent is started. The astronauts have only one chance to land.

Those watching on the ground heard two loud booms as the nose and tail of the shuttle broke the sound barrier about two minutes before touchdown. Then *Discovery* was visible as it approached the landing strip at the Kennedy Space Center. Gliding at 225 miles an hour, the shuttle's rear wheels touched the pavement, followed by the nose wheel. The waiting spectators gave a cheer as *Discovery* slowly rolled to a stop. STS-95 had been a perfect nine-day, 3.6-million-mile mission, followed by a perfect landing.

After landing, the astronauts had a long checklist to go through to shut down *Discovery*. They also had to get used to gravity again before they could walk out of the orbiter. Astronaut Roberta Bondar described what it feels like when they try to stand for the first time after a mission. "If you've ever been sick in bed for a week, you know that when you get up for the first time, your legs

The space shuttle Discovery *glides to a perfect landing at the Kennedy Space Center.*

are wobbly, your pulse is high, and you feel unsteady."[1] Those same feelings of dizziness and weakness affected the astronauts when they tried to move around after landing.

The *Discovery* crew stayed inside the orbiter a little longer than usual because John Glenn was vomiting. He later said, "I didn't feel so hot. I preloaded with too much fluid coming down."[2] He quickly recovered, though, and walked down the steps with the rest of the crew. They took a quick tour around the shuttle, inspecting the tiles and landing gear. Then the Crew Transport Vehicle took the astronauts back to the crew quarters.

After a brief medical examination, the seven *Discovery* astronauts were ready to see their family members. Waiting in the crowd was Annie Glenn, John Glenn's wife of fifty-five years. There were cheers as the astronauts stepped out of the elevator and into the arms of their loved ones. Hugs and kisses were exchanged while excited children danced around, grinning and laughing. The looks on the faces of the children brought to mind something John Glenn said a week before the mission.

John Glenn is reunited with his wife, Annie, after his historic space shuttle mission.

When I was a boy, like many children before and after me, I looked at the night sky and wondered what was out there and whether we could get there. Nobody at that time could have predicted, or even imagined, where we would be today. Yet we've achieved so much because people believed, experimented and persisted. They never took 'it can't be done' for an answer.[3]

CHAPTER NOTES

Chapter 1. Liftoff

1. NASA video feed of STS-95 launch, October 29, 1998.

2. Ann Hodges, "TV Coverage as Good as Last Time," *Houston Chronicle*, October 30, 1998, p. A21.

3. *NASA STS-95 Educational Downlink*, October 31, 1998, <http://38.201.67.77/shuttle/archives/sts-95/transcripts/fd3edutranscript.htm> (January 11, 1999).

4. Jim Schefter, "The Right Stuff—Again." *Popular Science*, May 1, 1998, p. 86.

5. *NASA STS-95 Educational Downlink*.

6. Roberta Bondar, *On the Shuttle* (New York: Firefly Books, 1993), p. 10.

7. Jeffrey Kluger, "Victory Lap," *Time*, November 11, 1998, p. 73.

Chapter 2. In Orbit

1. Jeffrey Kluger, "Victory Lap," *Time*, November 11, 1998, p. 73.

2. Ibid.

3. Mark Carreau, "Astronaut for the Ages Orbits Again," *Houston Chronicle*, October 30, 1998, p. A1.

4. Robert Crippen and John Young, "Our Phenomenal First Flight," *National Geographic*, October 1981, p. 494.

5. *NASA STS-95 Glenn/Brown News Conference*, November 5, 1998, <http://38.201.67.77/shuttle/archives/sts-95/transcripts/glenn_brown_conf.html> (March 16, 1999).

6. *NASA STS-95 US TV Networks Event,* November 2, 1998, <http://38.201.67.77/shuttle/archives/sts-95/transcripts ustvevent.html> (May 25, 1999).

7. *NASA STS-95 Glenn/Brown News Conference.*

8. Sally Ride, *To Space & Back* (New York: Lothrop, Lee & Shepard Books, 1986), p. 32.

9. R. Mike Mullane, *Do Your Ears Pop in Space?* (New York: John Wiley & Sons, Inc., 1997), p. 118.

Chapter 3. Eating, Cleaning, and Sleeping

1. Jeffrey Kluger, "Back to the Future," *Time,* August 17, 1998, p. 49.

2. *NASA STS-95 Educational Downlink,* October 31, 1998, <http://38.201.67.77/shuttle/archives/sts-95/transcripts/ fd3edutranscript.html> (January 11, 1999).

3. Ibid.

4. Mark Carreau, "Top Marks for Oldest Astronaut," *Houston Chronicle,* October 31, 1998, p. A1.

5. R. Mike Mullane, *Do Your Ears Pop in Space?* (New York: John Wiley & Sons, Inc., 1997), p. 107.

6. "Crew Answers Internet Questions During Flight," *STS Mission Profiles: STS-79,* July 1996, p. 34.

7. *NASA STS-95 US TV Networks Event,* November 2, 1998, <http://38.201.67.77/shuttle/archives/sts-95/transcripts ustvevent.html> (May 25, 1999).

8. *NASA STS-95 Educational Downlink.*

9. Mark Carreau, "Glenn Gives Students Something to Sleep On," *Houston Chronicle,* November 1, 1998, p. A12.

10. Mark Carreau, "80 Space Experiments on Agenda," *Houston Chronicle,* October 29, 1998, p. A9.

Chapter 4. Working and Relaxing

1. *NASA STS-95 Glenn/Brown News Conference,* November 5, 1998, <http://38.201.67.77/shuttle/archives/ sts-95/transcripts/glenn_brown_conf.html> (March 16, 1999).

2. *STS-95 Educational Downlink*, October 31, 1998, <http://38.201.67.77/shuttle/archives/sts-95/transcripts/fd3edutranscript.htm> (January 11, 1999).

3. William Newcott, "John Glenn: Man with a Mission," *National Geographic*, June 1999, p. 80.

4. NASA Press Briefing, August 15, 1998, Johnson Space Center.

5. Newcott, p. 68.

6. *NASA STS-95 Educational Downlink*.

7. Ibid.

8. Mark Carreau, "Glenn Has Globs of Fun in Space," *Houston Chronicle*, November 3, 1998, p. A2.

9. Mark Carreau, "Shuttle Crew Retrieves Observatory Satellite," *Houston Chronicle*, November 4, 1998, p. A5.

Chapter 5. Return to Earth

1. Roberta Bondar, *On the Shuttle* (New York: Firefly Books, 1993), p. 61.

2. "Glenn Suffered Nauseous Attack," *Houston Chronicle*, December 12, 1998, p. A2.

3. John Glenn, "Why We Must Venture into Space," *Parade Magazine*, October 25, 1998, p. 7.

GLOSSARY

accelerate—To move faster or gain speed.

airlock—An airtight chamber that separates the pressurized interior of a spacecraft from the vacuum of space.

atmosphere—The gas surrounding a planet, such as the mass of air surrounding Earth.

cockpit—The area in an aircraft for the pilot.

corona—The layer of gas surrounding the Sun.

crystal—A substance in which the particles are arranged in a regular, repeating pattern.

diabetic—A person who has diabetes, a disease in which the body is not able to break down blood sugar.

environment—A person's surroundings.

friction—The rubbing of one object against another.

ignition—The act of causing a fuel mixture to burn.

inferno—Great heat or flames.

insulin—A hormone made by the pancreas.

jettison—To throw overboard or discard.

orbit—The path taken by one object around another, such as the Moon around Earth.

orbiter—Another name for the space shuttle.

payload bay—The large area of the space shuttle that is used to carry cargo, such as satellites, into orbit.

plasma—The fluid part of the blood.

robotic arm—A fifty-foot-long tool used to move objects in and out of the space shuttle's payload bay.

satellite—A celestial body or object orbiting around another larger body. The Spartan satellite orbited Earth.

sensors—A device that measures or records data.

solar—Having to do with the Sun.

Spacehab—A portable laboratory module that can be added to the space shuttle's payload bay for some missions.

space shuttle—The first reusable spacecraft that carries astronauts and equipment into orbit; designed with wings so it can glide back to Earth.

stow—To put away for future use.

weightless—Having little or no apparent weight.

FURTHER READING

Books

Berliner, Don. *Living in Space*. Minneapolis: The Lerner Publishing Group, 1993.

Bredeson, Carmen. *Gus Grissom: A Space Biography*. Springfield, N.J.: Enslow Publishers, Inc., 1998.

————. *Our Space Program*. Brookfield, Conn.: Millbrook Press, Inc., 1999.

Campbell, Ann-Jeanette. *Amazing Space: A Book of Answers for Kids*. New York: John Wiley & Sons, Inc., 1997.

Cole, Michael D. *Friendship 7: First American in Orbit*. Springfield, N.J.: Enslow Publishers, Inc., 1995.

Mullane, R. Mike. *Do Your Ears Pop in Space?* New York: John Wiley & Sons, Inc., 1997.

Vogt, Gregory. *The Space Shuttle*. Brookfield, Conn.: Millbrook Press, Inc., 1991.

Internet Addresses

Dunbar, Brian. *NASA Homepage.* "Search the NASA Web." September 13, 1999. <http://www.nasa.gov/> (September 13, 1999).

Johnson Space Center. "Earth from Space." August 26, 1999. <http://earth.jsc.nasa.gov/> (August 26, 1999).

National Aeronautics and Space Administration. *NASA Human Spaceflight.* September 10, 1999. <http://shuttle.nasa.gov/> (September 13, 1999).

National Aeronautics and Space Administration. *SpaceLink.* n.d. <http://spacelink.msfc.nasa.gov/> (September 13, 1999).

INDEX